How Many Can You See?

by Anne Diorio

I like animals.

Look at all my animals.

How many elephants can you see?

How many horses can you see?

How many elephants and horses do I have?

5 + 3 = ?

I have lots of buttons!

Can you see eight red buttons?

Can you see four blue buttons?

How many red and blue buttons do I have?

8 + 4 = ?

Now look at my hats.
I have five caps.
I have two top hats.

How many caps and top hats do I have?

5 + 2 = ?

I like cats! How many orange cats do I have? How many black cats do I have?

How many caps and top hats do I have?

5 + 2 = ?

I like cats! How many orange cats do I have? How many black cats do I have?

Can you see four pens?

Can you see two pencils?

How many pens and pencils do I have?

4 + 2 = ?

I like little boxes.

I have three purple boxes.

I have one blue box.

Can you see them?

3 + 1 = ?

I like paper cranes.

I have four yellow cranes.

I have one green crane.

How many yellow and green cranes do I have?

4 + 1 = ?

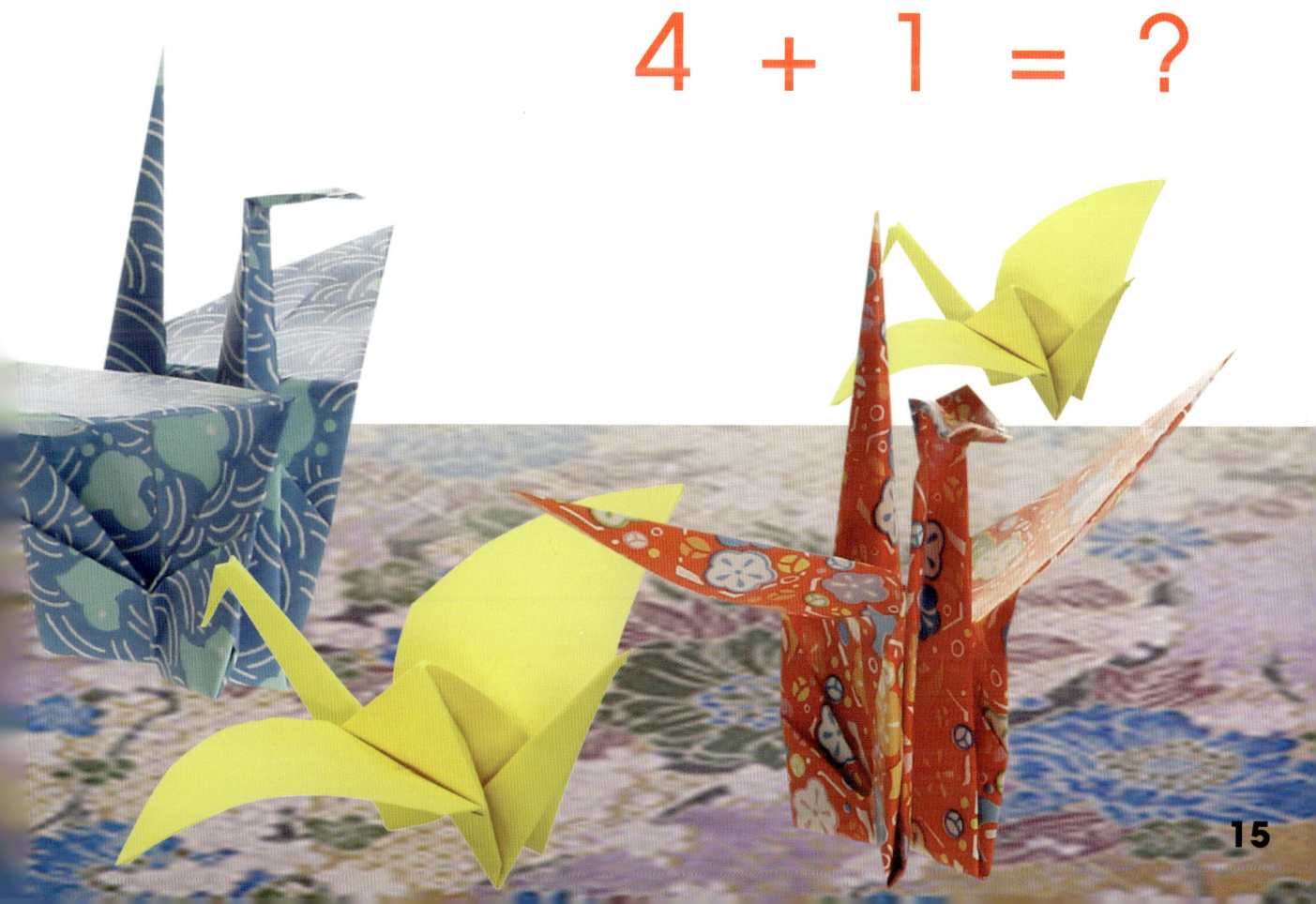

I like the green crane the best!